W9-BAH-308

My Beastly Book of Tangled Tinsel

Also in this series

Owlkids Books Inc.
10 Lower Spadina Avenue, Suite 400, Toronto, Ontario M5V 2Z2
www.owlkidsbooks.com

North America edition © 2012 Owlkids Books Inc.

Illustrations © 2011 Christine Roussey
Translation: Angela Keenlyside

Published in France under the title *Mon cahier de Noël* © 2011
Éditions Milan, 300 rue Léon-Joulin, 31101 Toulouse Cedex 9
www.editionsmilan.com

All rights reserved. No part of this book may be reproduced or copied in any form
without written consent from the publisher.

Distributed in Canada by University of Toronto Press
5201 Dufferin Street, Toronto, Ontario M3H 5T8

Distributed in the United States by Publishers Group West
1700 Fourth Street, Berkeley, California 94710

Library and Archives Canada Cataloguing in Publication

Roussey, Christine
    My beastly book of tangled tinsel : 140 ways to doodle,
scribble, color and draw / illustrated by Christine Roussey.

Translation of: Mon cahier de Noël.
ISBN 978-1-926973-55-5

    1. Christmas in art--Juvenile literature.
2. Drawing--Technique--Juvenile literature. I. Title.

NC825.C49R68 2012   j743'.893942663   C2012-900376-X

Library of Congress Control Number: 2012931134

Canadian Heritage   Patrimoine canadien

Canada

Ontario
Ontario Media Development Corporation
Société de développement de l'industrie des médias de l'Ontario

Canada Council for the Arts   Conseil des Arts du Canada

ONTARIO ARTS COUNCIL
CONSEIL DES ARTS DE L'ONTARIO

We acknowledge the financial support of the Canada Council for the Arts, the Ontario Arts Council,
the Government of Canada through the Canada Book Fund (CBF) and the Government of Ontario
through the Ontario Media Development Corporation's Book Initiative for our publishing activities.

Manufactured by C & C Offset Printing Co.
Manufactured in Shenzhen, China, in June 2012
Job #2012-01108

A   B   C   D   E   F

Publisher of Chirp, chickaDEE and OWL
www.owlkids.com

'Twas the night before Christmas…
And Santa's reindeer were tired,
His suit was ripped,
And the carolers were out of tune.

Fix things however you want!
Just grab your markers, colored pencils, scissors, glue, and tape.

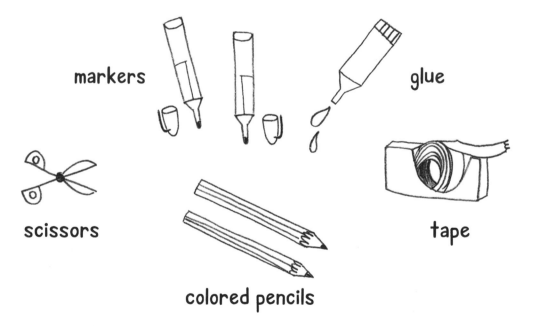

markers

glue

scissors

colored pencils

tape

Follow each instruction and let your imagination go!

Happy Holidays!

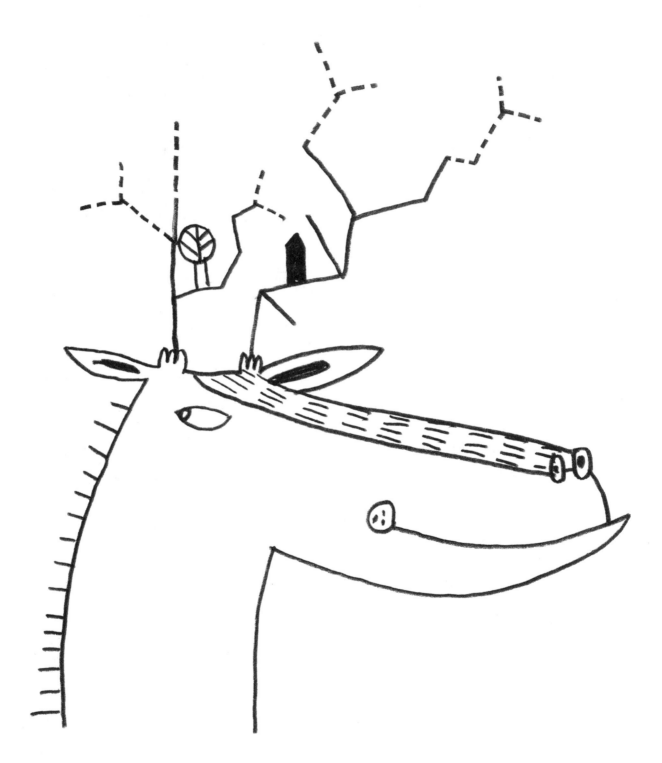

This reindeer is missing something.
Give him **antlers** as long and as twisted as possible!

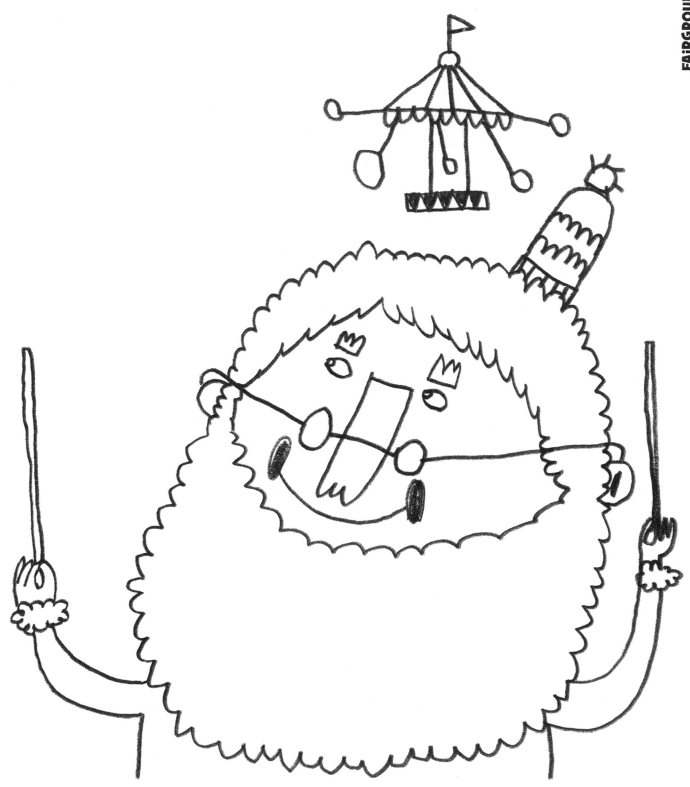

Draw **cotton candy** for Santa Claus.

Decorate your favorite tree in the **forest**.

Were you nice this year?
Draw yourself under the halo.

Finish the curls of the **ribbons**
and color the wrapping paper.

Decorate this **sign** nicely,
then cut it out and stick it to your front door.

Tired of fir trees? Finish drawing the Christmas **palm tree**.

Find and circle the **7** differences between **Leon** and Santa Claus.

Add 3 more of your own.

Santa's sister and her puppy aren't ready for Christmas!
Decorate them like **Christmas trees**.

CHRISTMAS EVERY DAY!
MEGA-IMPORTANT PETITION

Name

Signature

Cut out this page and sign the **petition**
to make it Christmas every day.

Sick of snowmen?
Draw a snow **goat**.

Draw **funny faces** on Santa's old family photo
and color their holiday sweaters.

Color the sky black so that **night** will fall
and Santa will come.

The lights on the tree are burnt out.
Color everything black.

Dear Santa Claus,

Write a **letter** to Santa Claus. Cut out this page
and glue on pictures of the presents of your dreams.

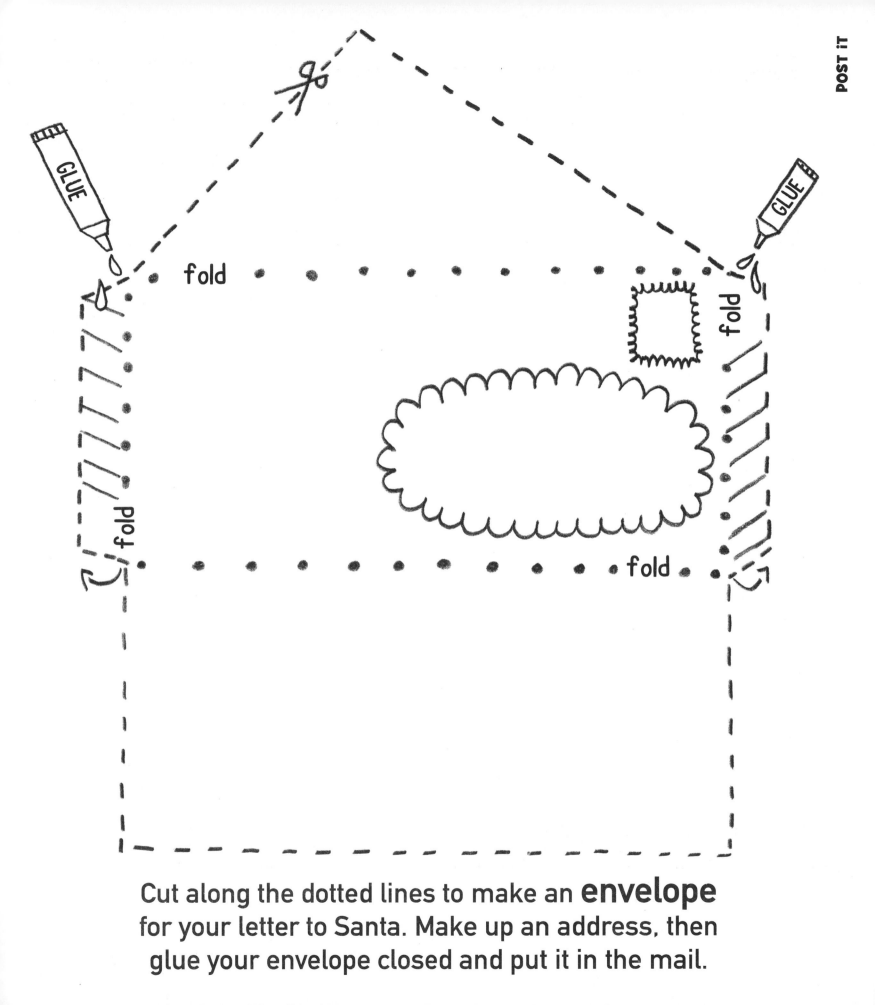

GLUE

GLUE

fold

fold

fold

fold

Cut along the dotted lines to make an envelope for your letter to Santa. Make up an address, then glue your envelope closed and put it in the mail.

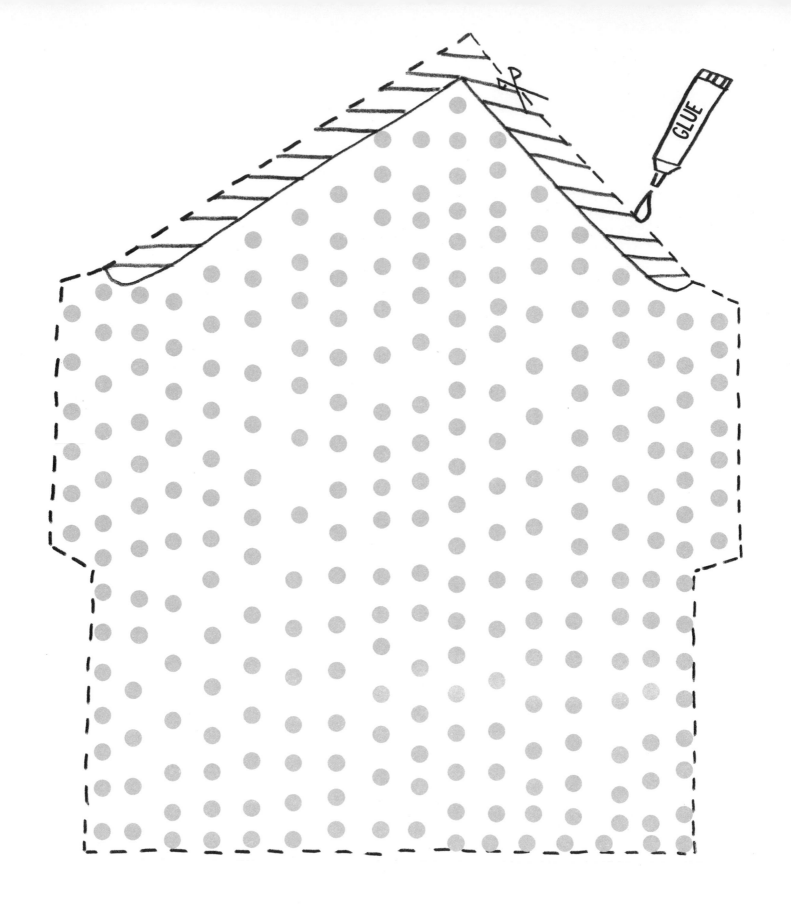

Glue your photo to the page or draw your **face** in the open space.

Finish the second half of the tree and color it **pink**.

Here is Santa's bedroom.
Connect the dots to discover his **hero**.

TOY BAND

Color the lovely Christmas window **display**.

Draw the most **dreadful** present possible.

Draw the **best** present ever.

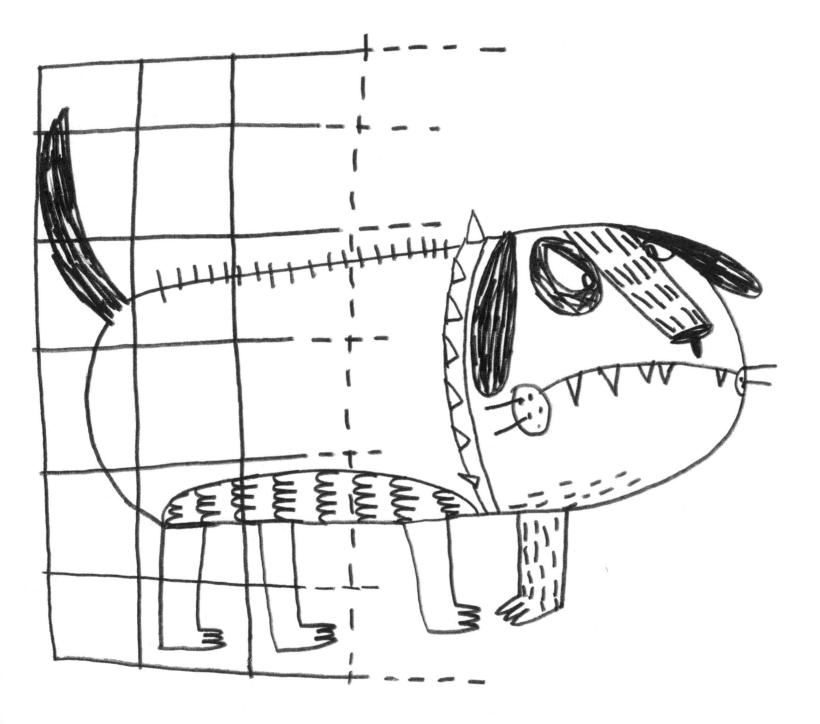

Finish the kennel for **Buddy**, the neighbor's dog,
so he goes to sleep before Santa arrives.

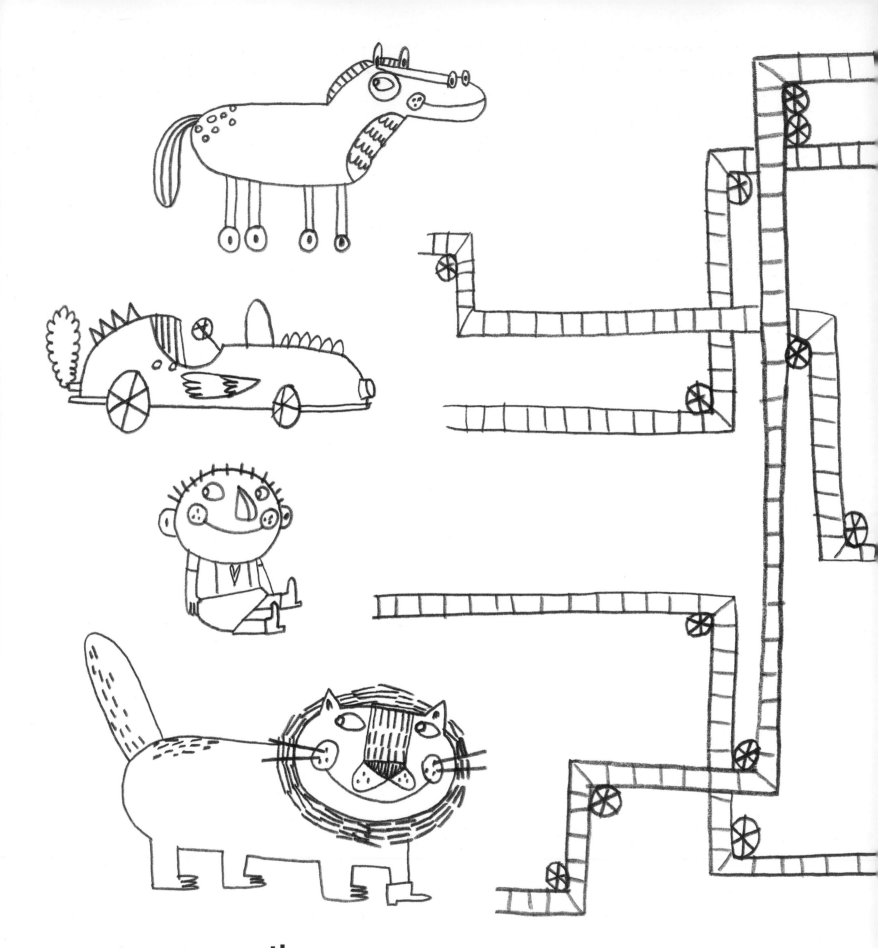

Follow the right **paths** to connect the toys with their proper boxes.

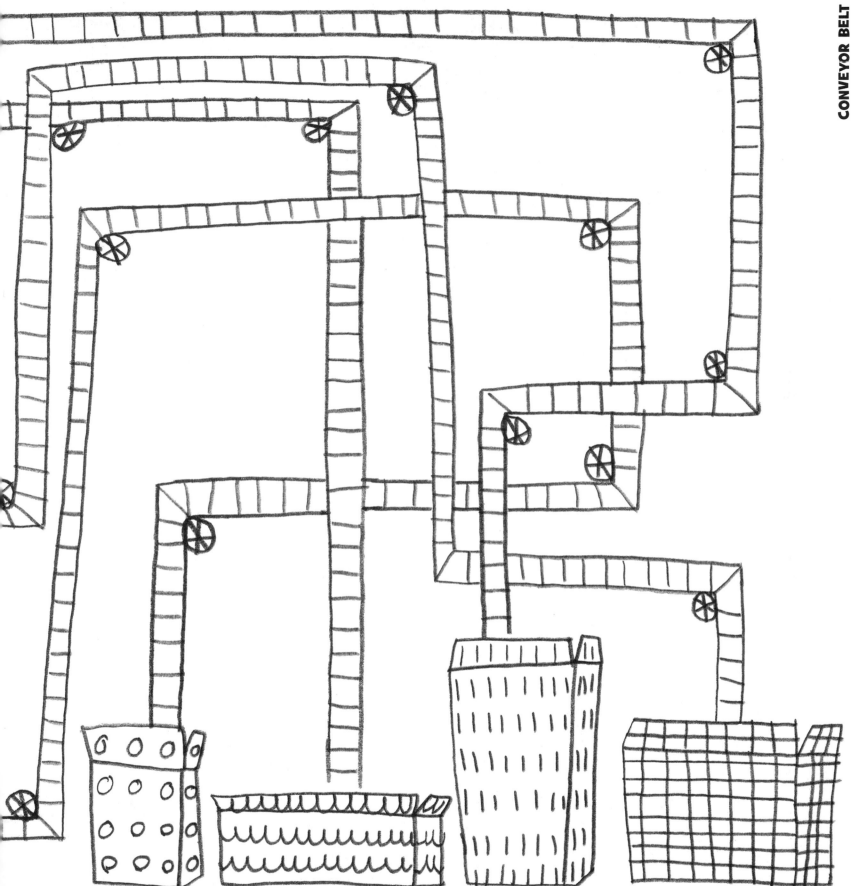

Block the **chimneys** of the naughty children
so they can't get their presents.

Find the real Santa among all the **imposters** and color him.

Reindeer **fashion show**!

Color the outfits in your least favorite colors.

Santa Claus

Mrs. Claus

Daughter

Son

Snowman

Dog

Reindeer

This is Santa's family.
Draw each of them in a Christmas **hat**.

Who is this? Color their hair grey,
their hat red, and turn the page to find out…

It's Mrs. Claus and her dog. What a **joker**...

Cut out this **calendar** and post it in your kitchen.
Cross out the days until Christmas.

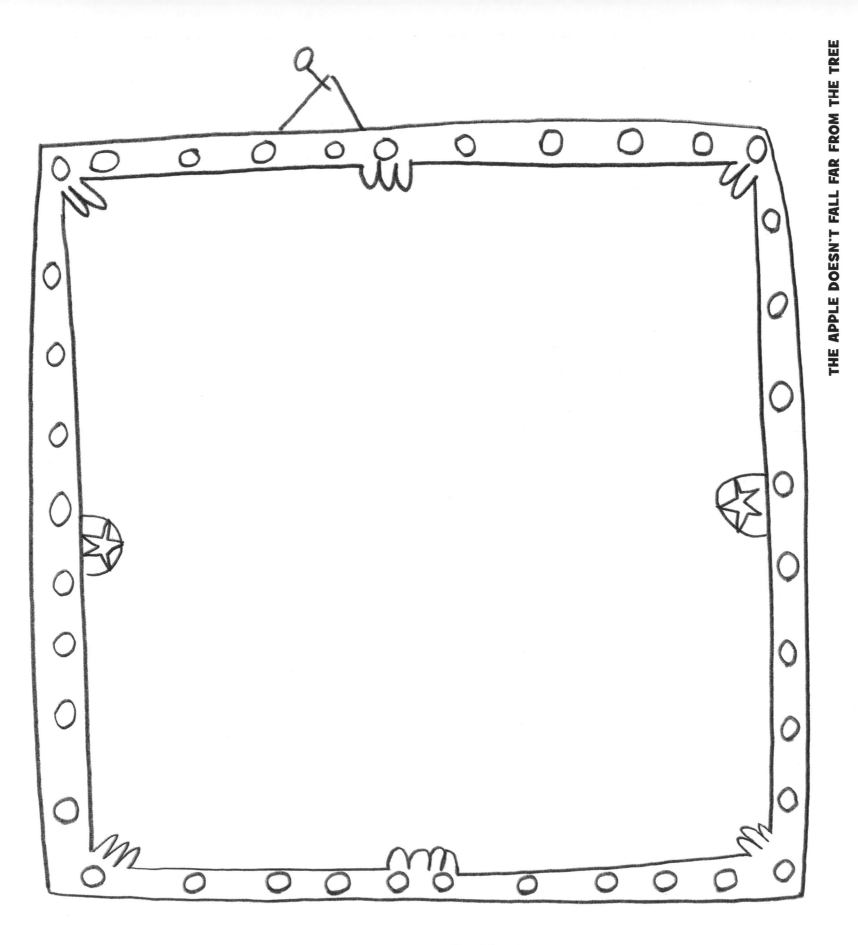

Draw Santa's **father**.

Hurray! It's Christmas **morning**!

Color the lamps to turn them on, draw the sun in the sky, and open the eyes of the well-behaved children.

Connect the dots to discover Santa's cool **carriage**.

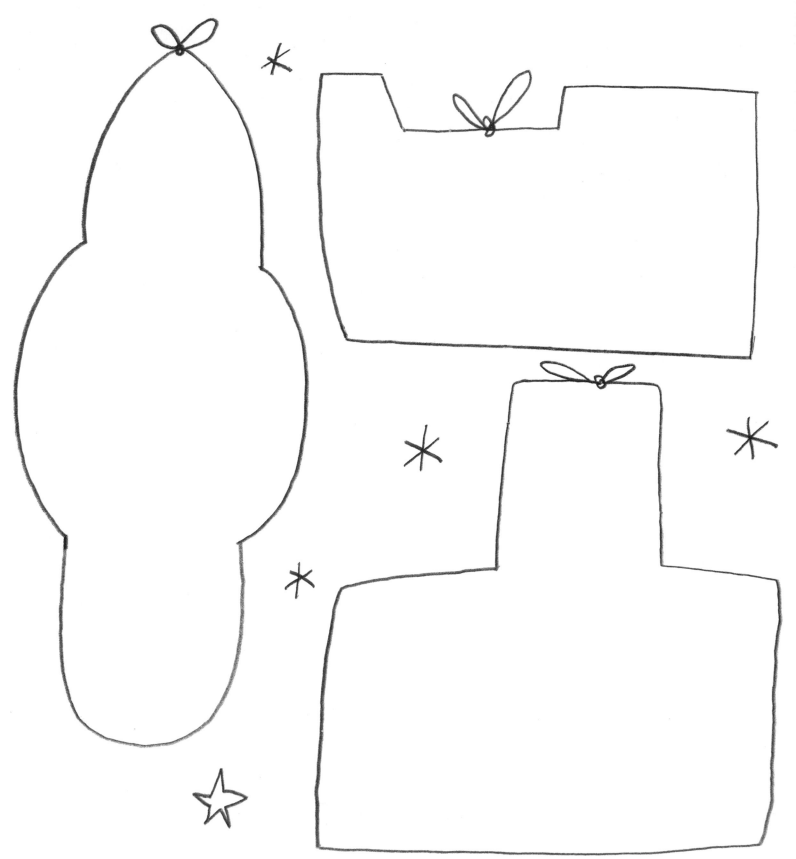

Draw what might be inside these **parcels**.
Then turn the page to see if you guessed correctly.

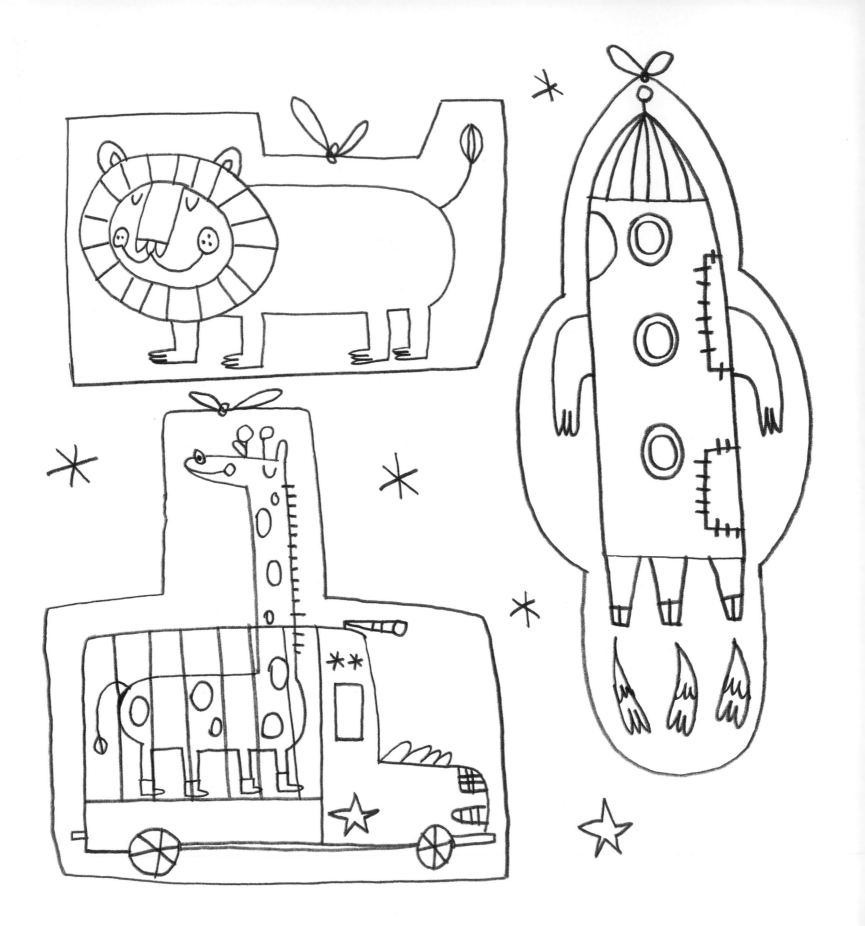

Which shoes are yours? Add lots of presents to your pile.

Circle the **toys** you hope to find in Santa's sack.

Color and cut out your favorite **decorations**.

Glue your decorations to the front of the **building**.

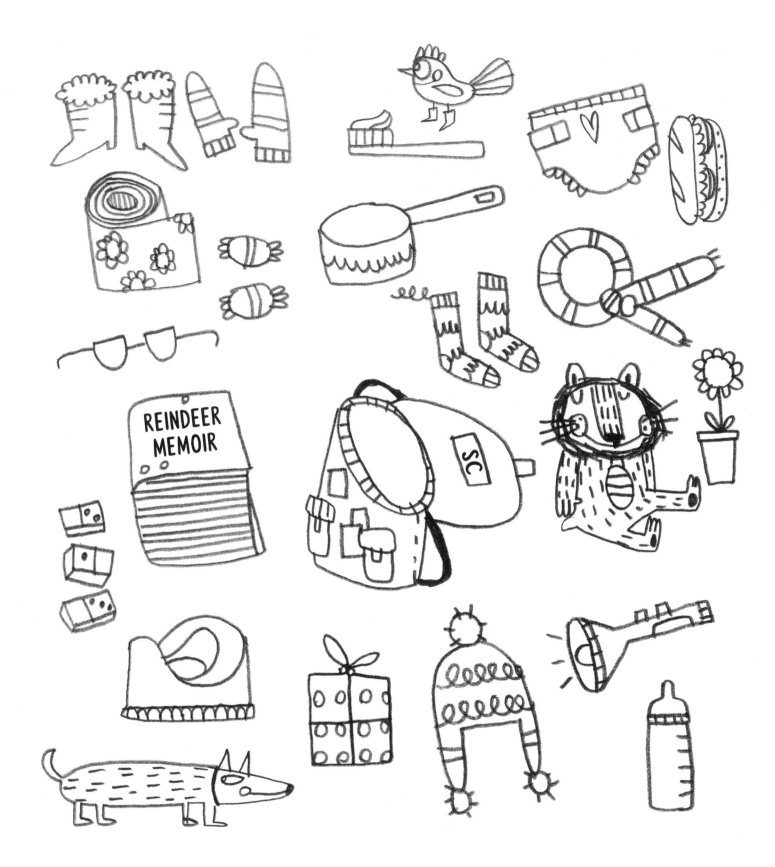

Help Santa prepare for his long night.
Color the things he needs to bring with him in his **bag**.

Connect each gift to its matching **shoe**.

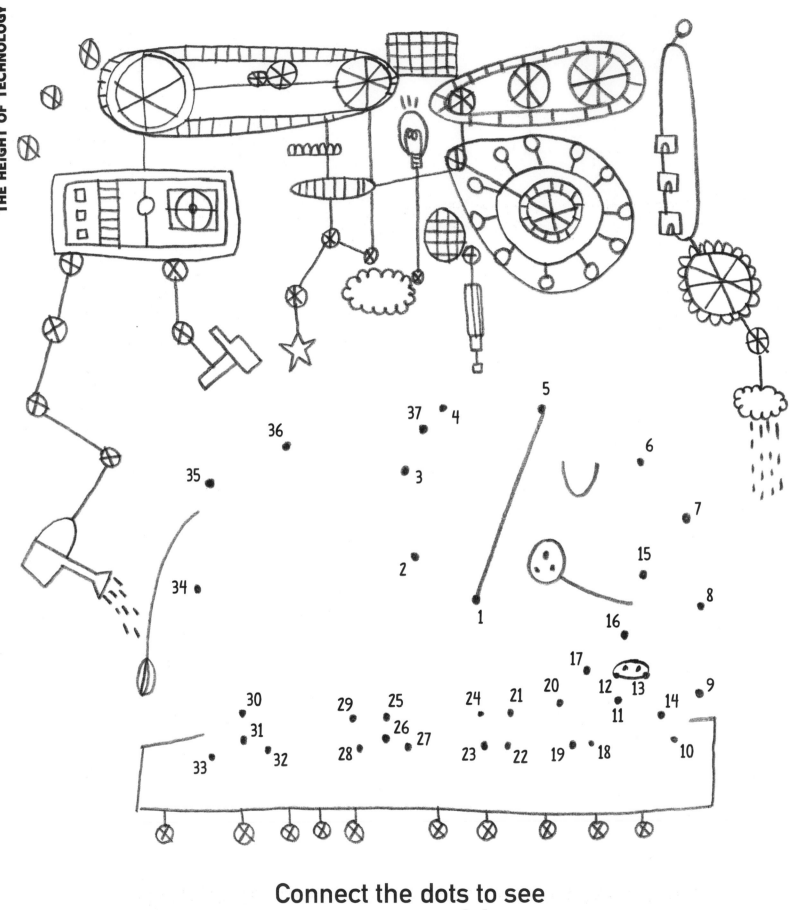

Connect the dots to see
what the **present machine** is making.

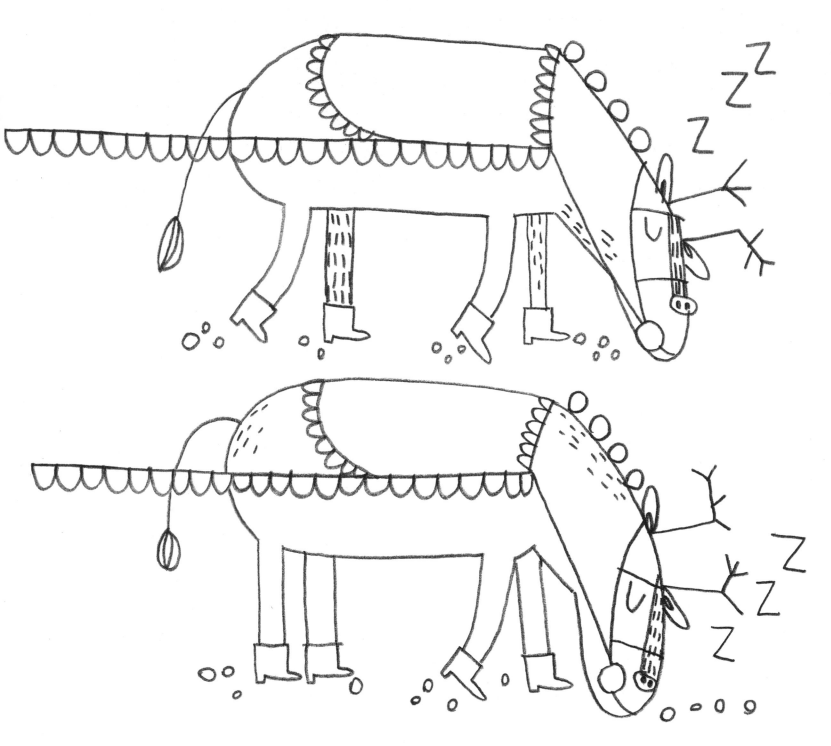

Draw food for the reindeer to give them **energy**.
Turn the page to see what happens.

Draw a new costume for Santa Claus.

Spot the present that doesn't belong.
What do you think it is?

Santa is as big as the house!
Draw **tiny** people sleeping in this tiny house.

It's **Christmas Eve**.
How many Santas can you count in the picture?

Color all the Santas, but circle the real one.

Santa is on **vacation**.
Can you recognize him?

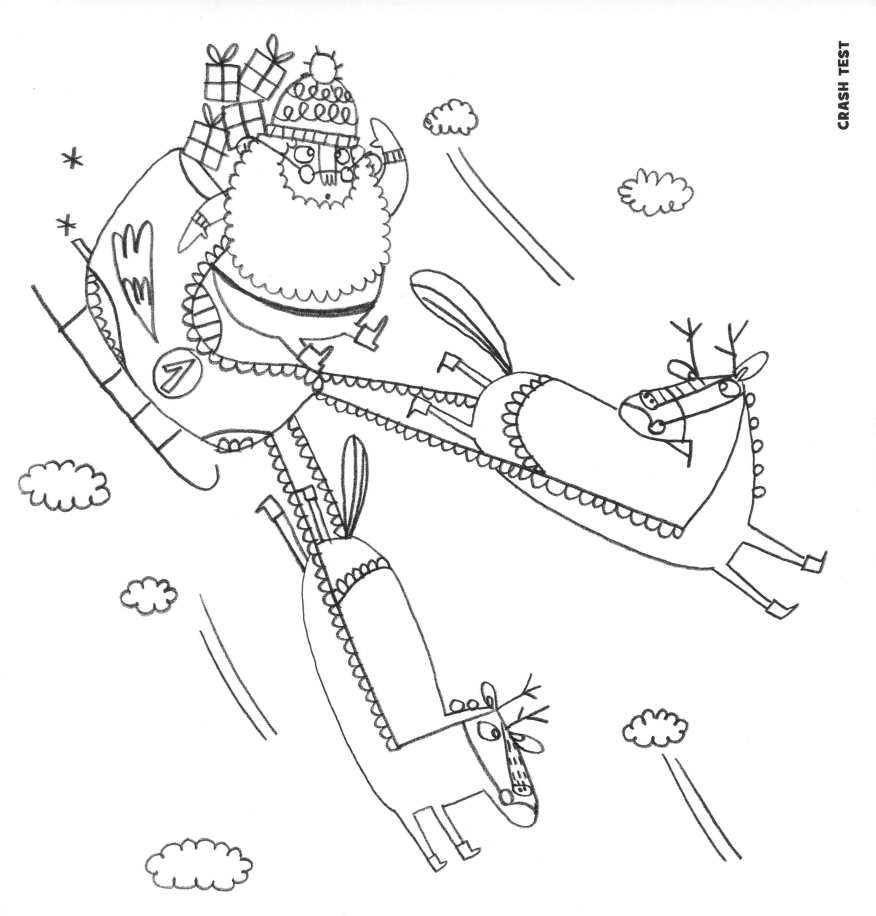

Out of practice!
Quick, draw **wings** on the reindeer.

Help Santa jump from roof to roof.

Continue drawing his path.

Draw a **gingerbread woman**
decorated with leftovers from Christmas dinner.

Oh no! Santa fell in the **holly**!
Cut the page to remove the thorns.

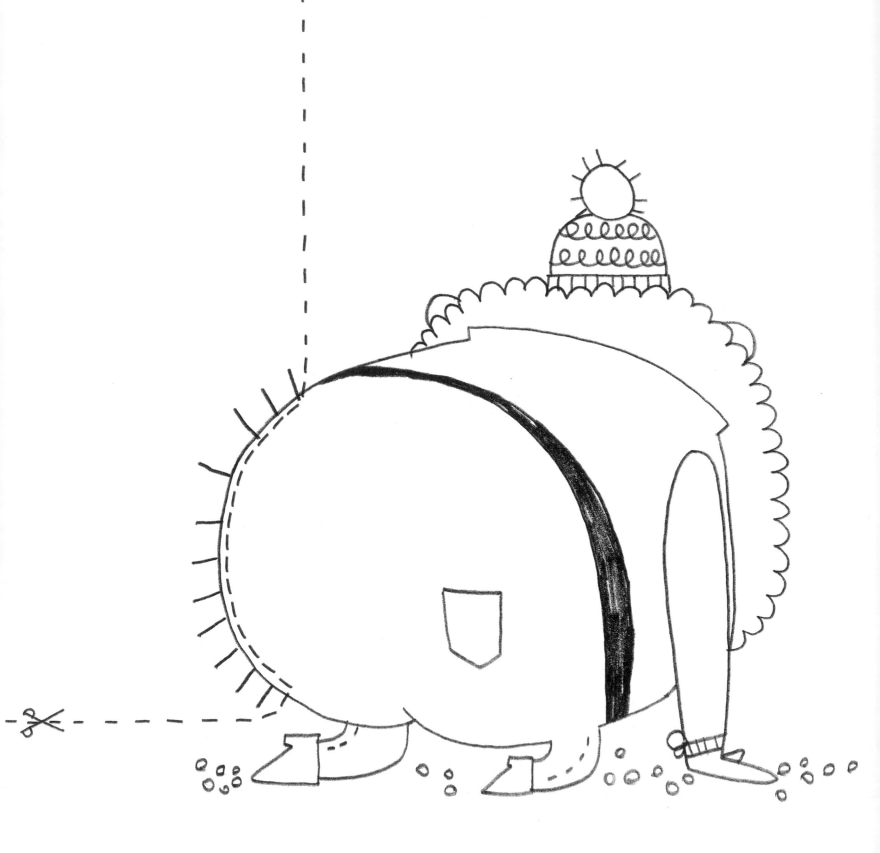

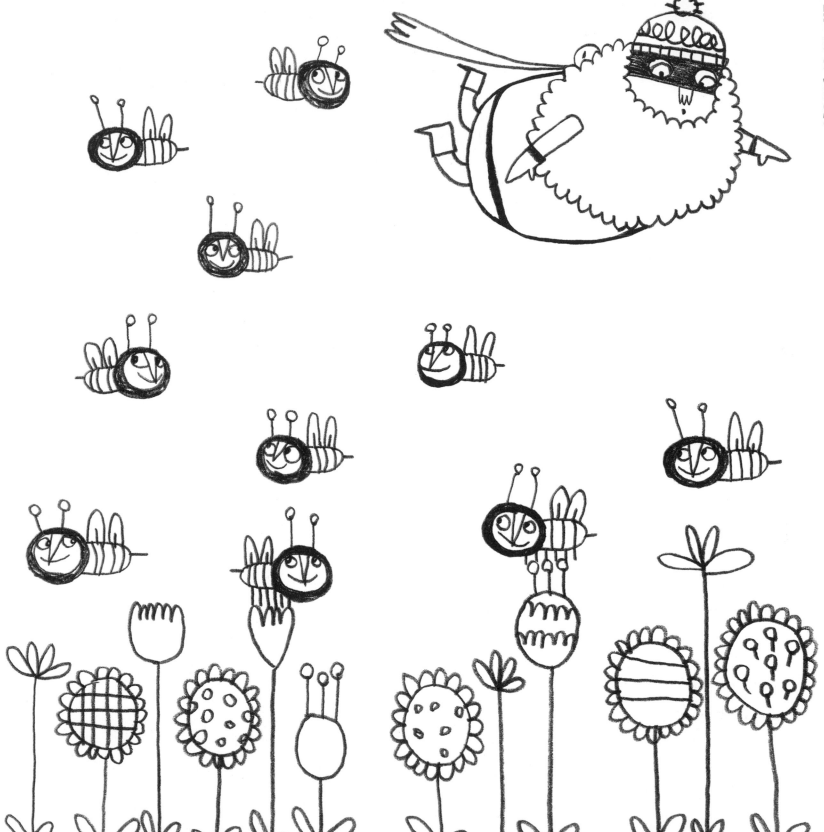

Camouflage! Color the bees and Santa black and yellow.

A practical joker has hidden Santa's **hat** in his bedroom. Find it and color everything except the hat.

Brrr! Finish coloring
the **flames** in the fireplace to light the fire.

Draw Santa a path to the good little **boy**.

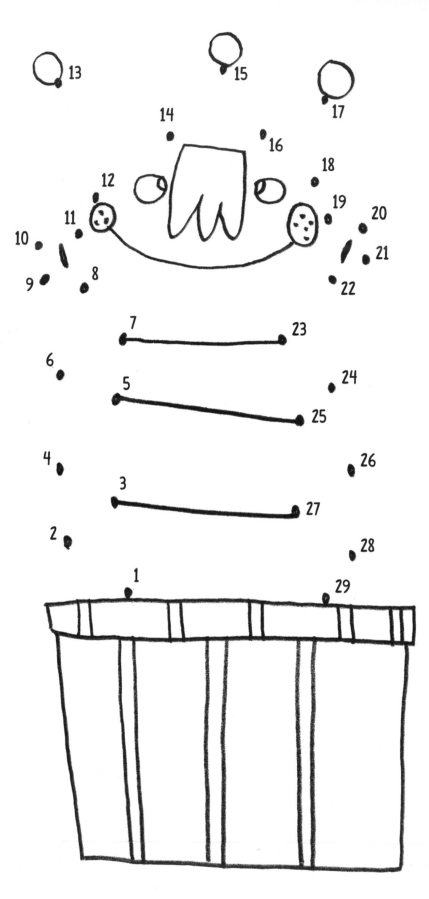

Hurray, a present! Connect the dots to discover the **surprise** inside.

Draw a **penguin** and a **polar bear**
dressed like Mr. and Mrs. Claus.

Trace the dotted lines and finish the **trees**.

Decorate each one without using red or green.

Surprise! Draw what these **children** got for Christmas.

Connect the dots to trap the present **thief**.

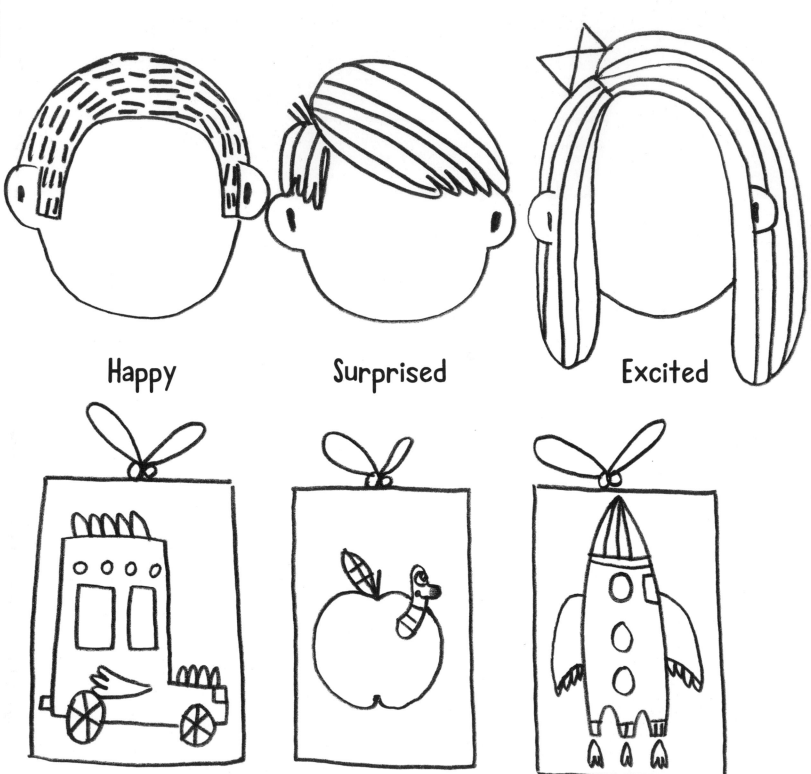

Happy   Surprised   Excited

Draw the **expressions** of the children as they open their presents.

Draw dreadful, **rotten** decay on
the spoiled-rotten teeth of the spoiled-rotten children.

Draw three **giant** elves
and one tiny elf parading around the tree.

Color and cut out the **ornaments**. Make a
small hole in the top for a thread and decorate your tree.

Santa went down a **chimney**.
Cover him in soot with a black crayon.

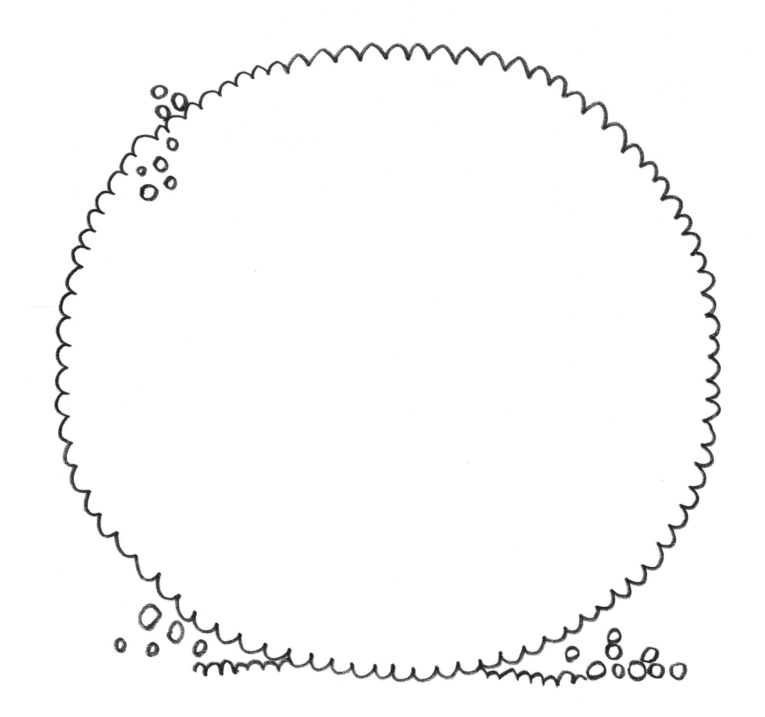

Draw a **ferocious** face on this snow monster's head.

It's freezing! Draw frozen **boogers** on Santa.

Draw a **yeti** dressed in its Christmas best.

Warm up by the fire!
Draw your face in the open space and color the scene.

Kids in the Old West need to be spoiled too!
Draw a **cowboy hat** on Santa.

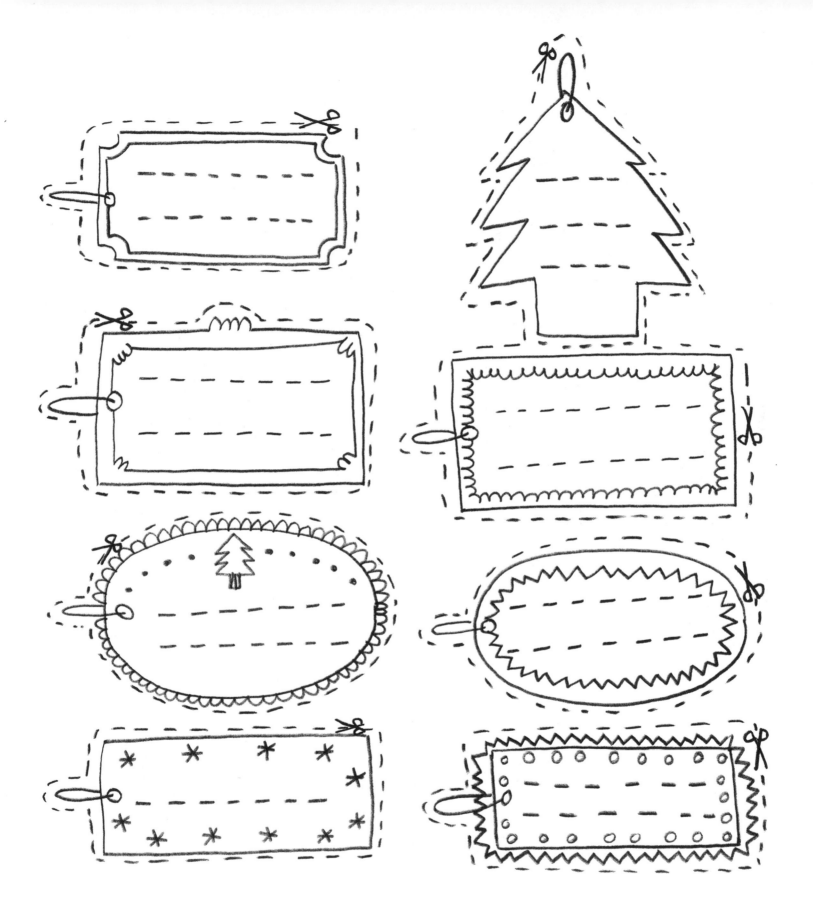

Santa was here! Write your name on all the **gift tags**
and stick them to all the presents under your tree.

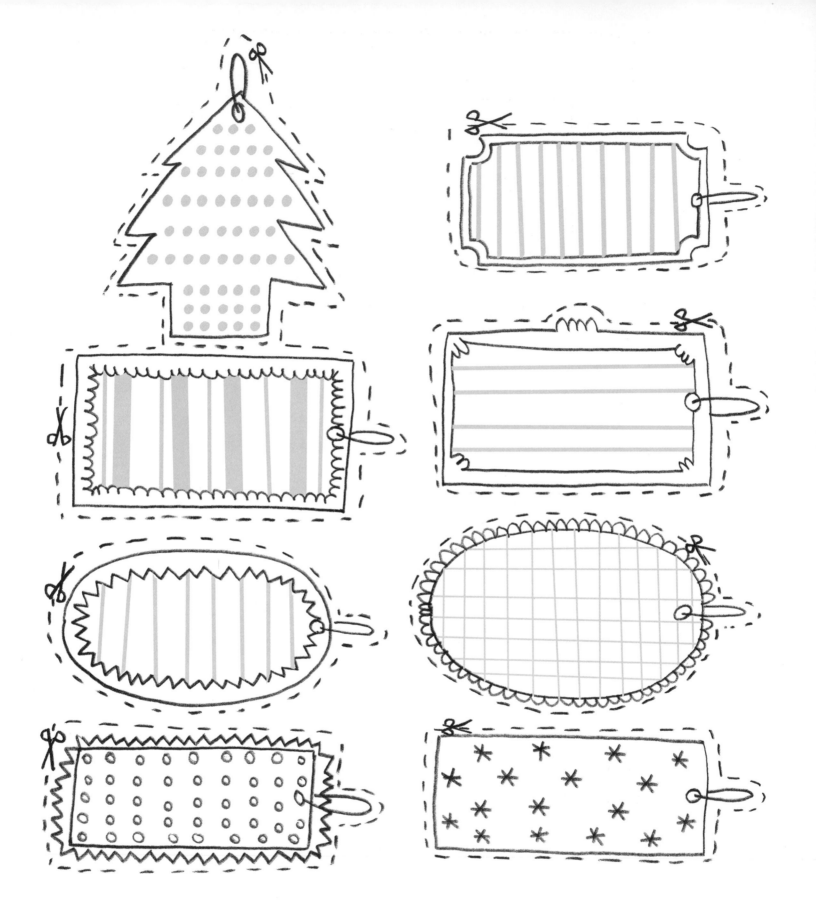

Hold on, there's a knock at the **door**. Turn the page to open it.

Oh no! It's not Santa—it's Uncle Albert.
Color him **green**.

FINISH

A winding trail! With a **marker** in each hand,
help Santa and his sleigh find the fastest route through the forest.

The **choir** is horrible! Throw tomatoes and rotten pears at them.

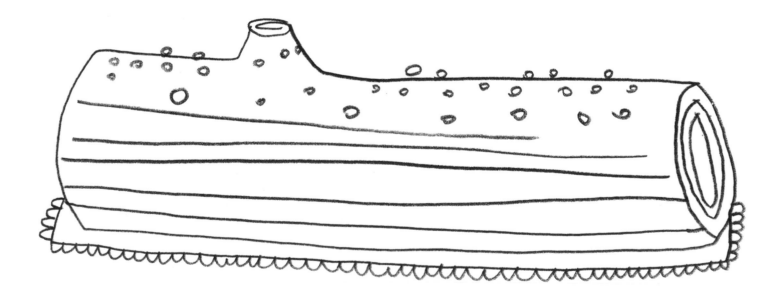

Yum-yum! Choose some decorations
and redraw them on the **chocolate** log.

Draw the **baby** of a snowman and a reindeer.

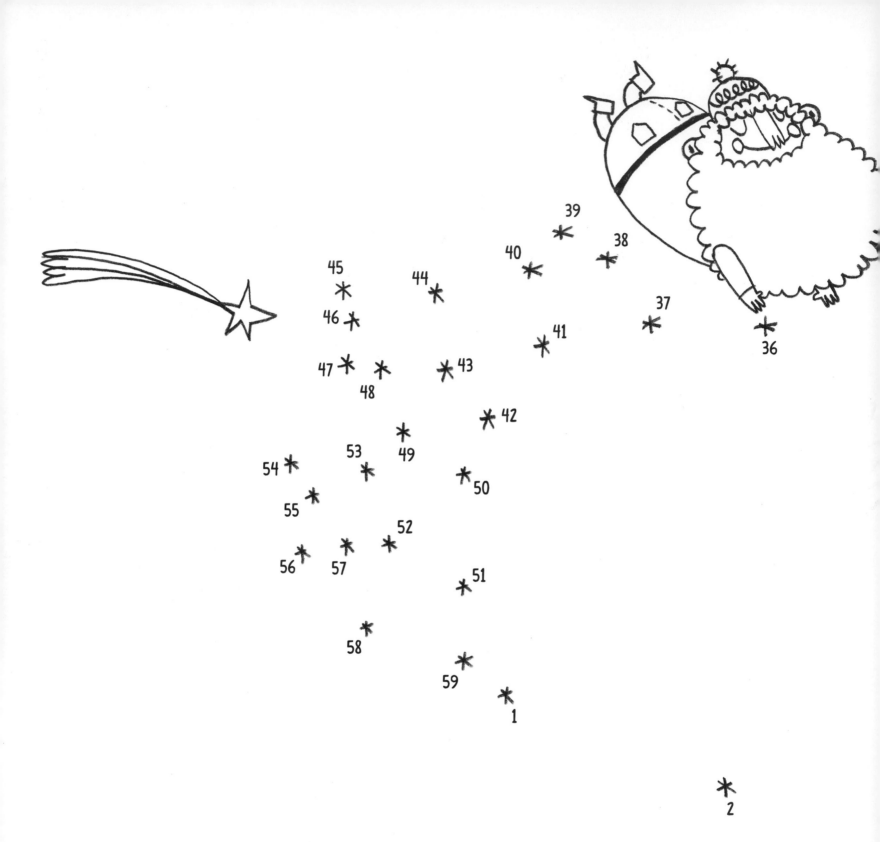

A falling star! Santa made a **wish**.

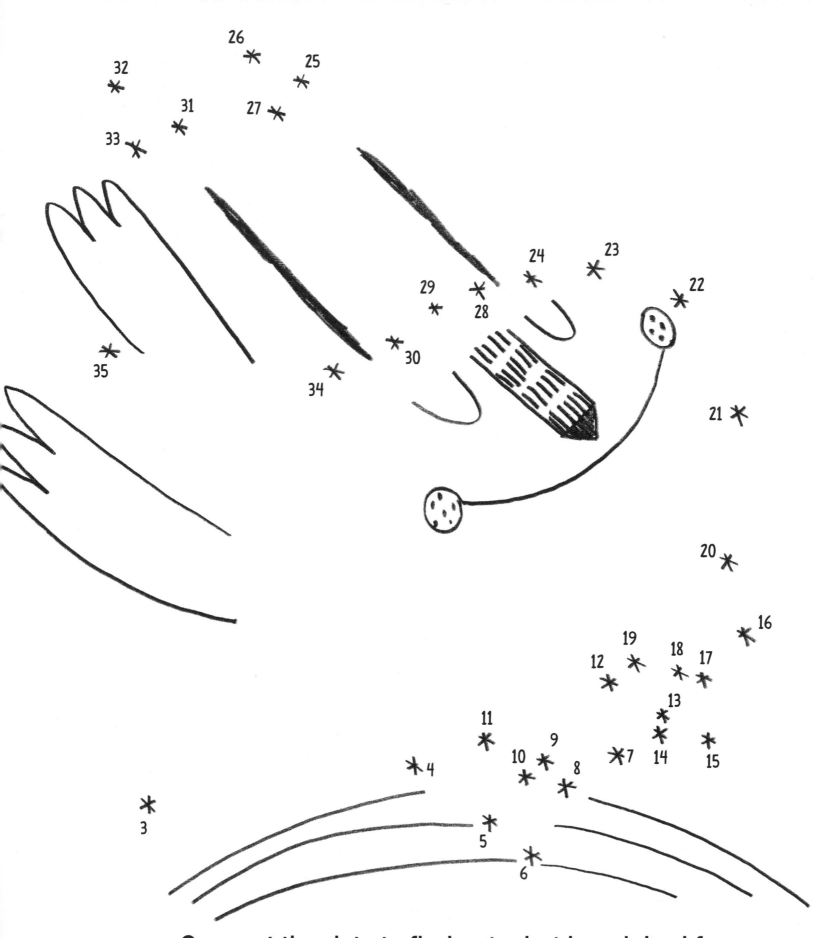

Connect the dots to find out what he wished for.

Santa lost his **pants**.
Draw him another pair.

If you were Santa, what would you wear?
Draw your **dream suit** here.

In your opinion, who is the **fastest**?

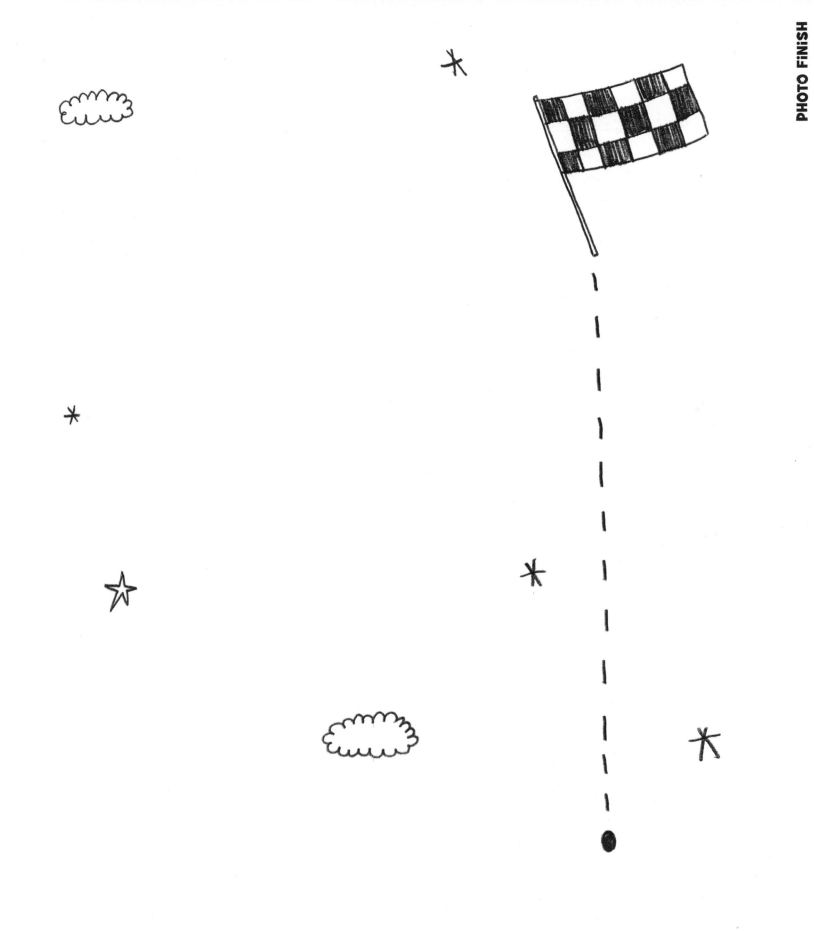

Draw the winner passing the finish line.

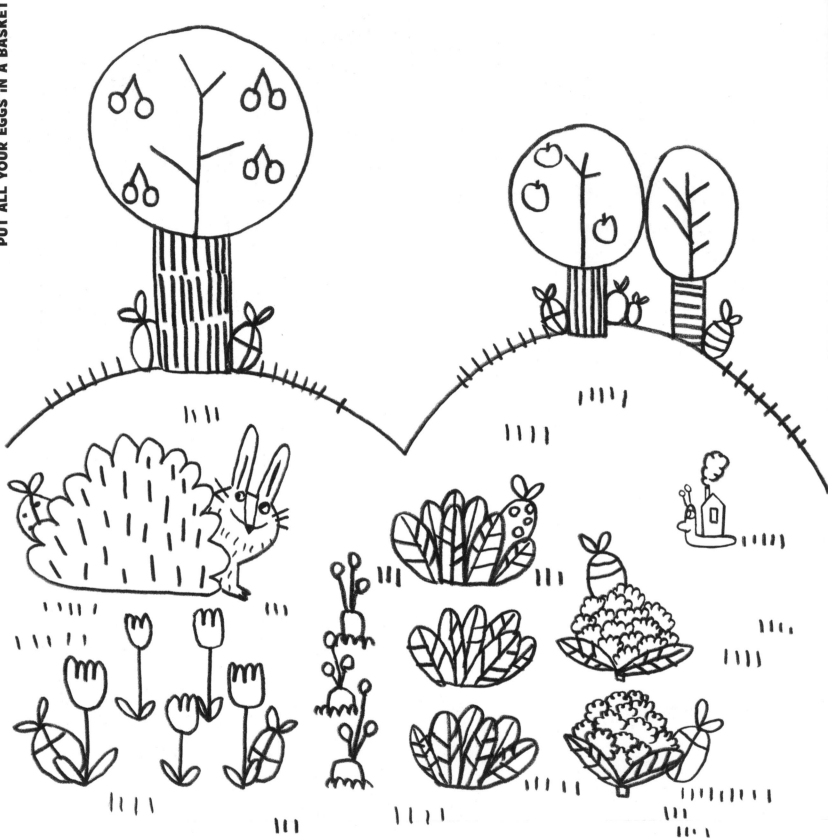

Sick of Christmas? Find the Easter **eggs**
hiding in the garden and color them. Don't use red or green!

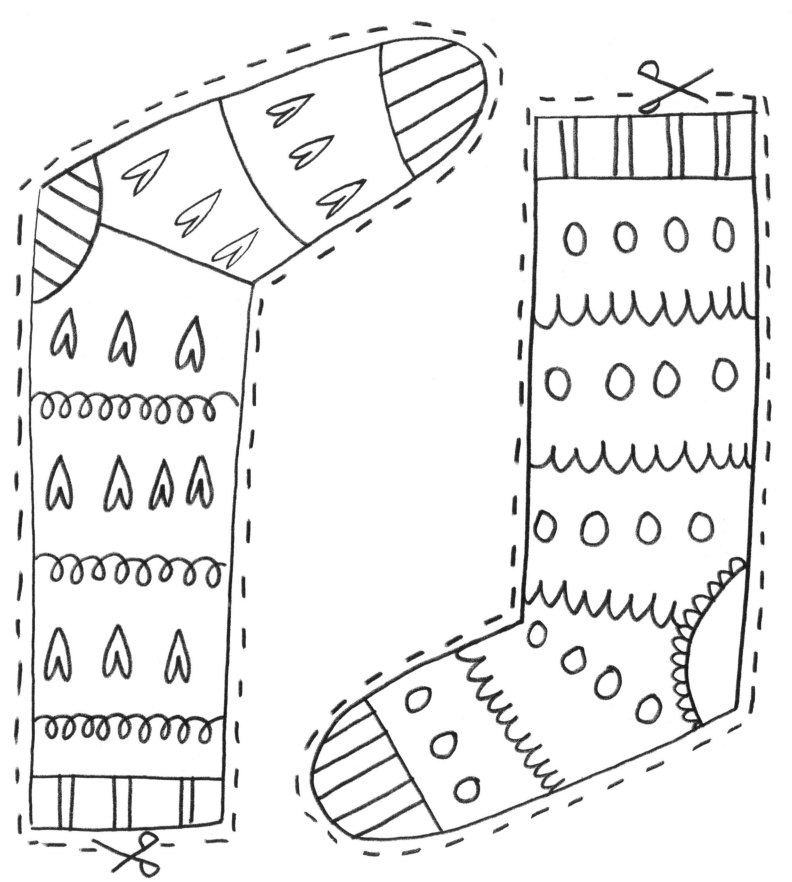

Color and cut out the stockings to decorate your house.

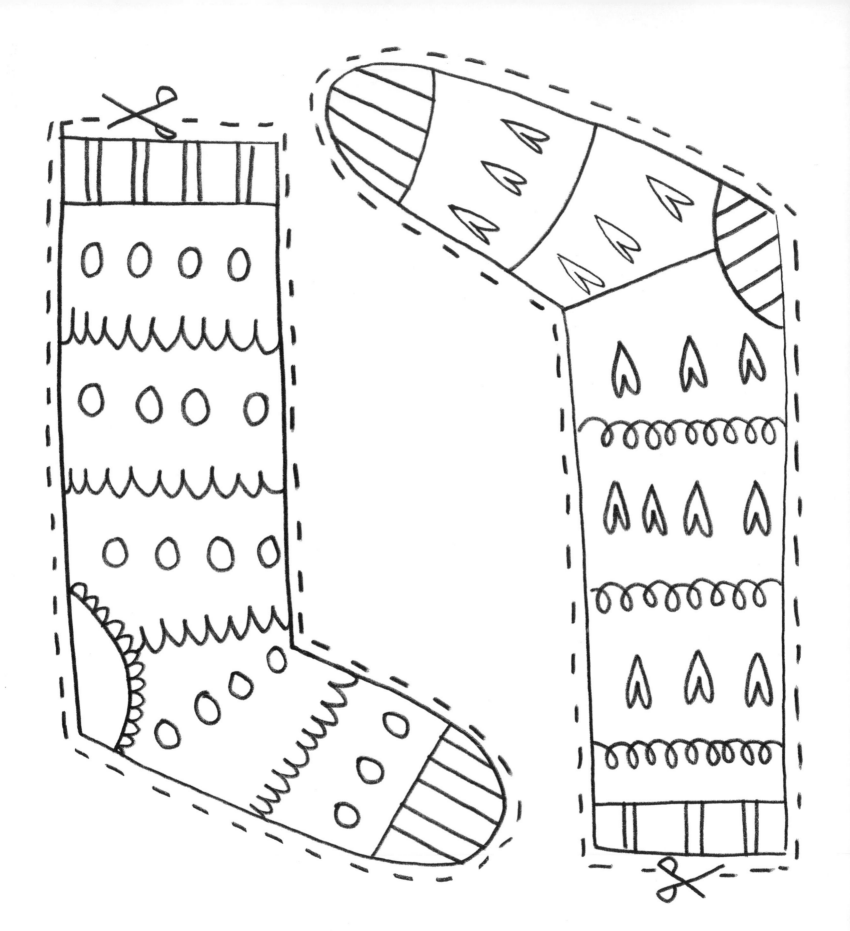

It's not always Christmas…
Close this book and **clean** your room.

Imagine the **dinner** of your dreams.

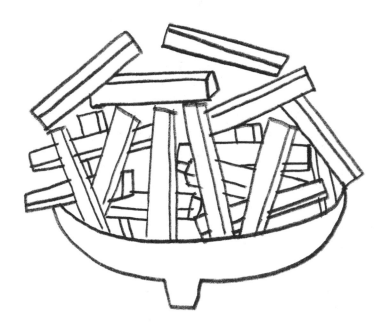

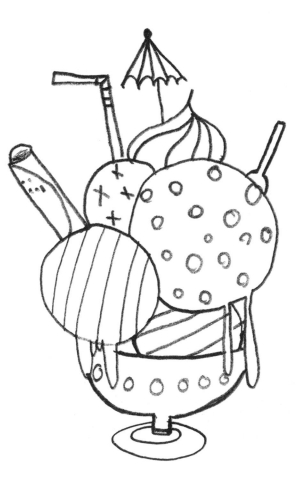

Cross out what you don't like and color what you would like to eat.

The **reindeer** are tired.
Finish drawing the clouds under their feet so they can rest.

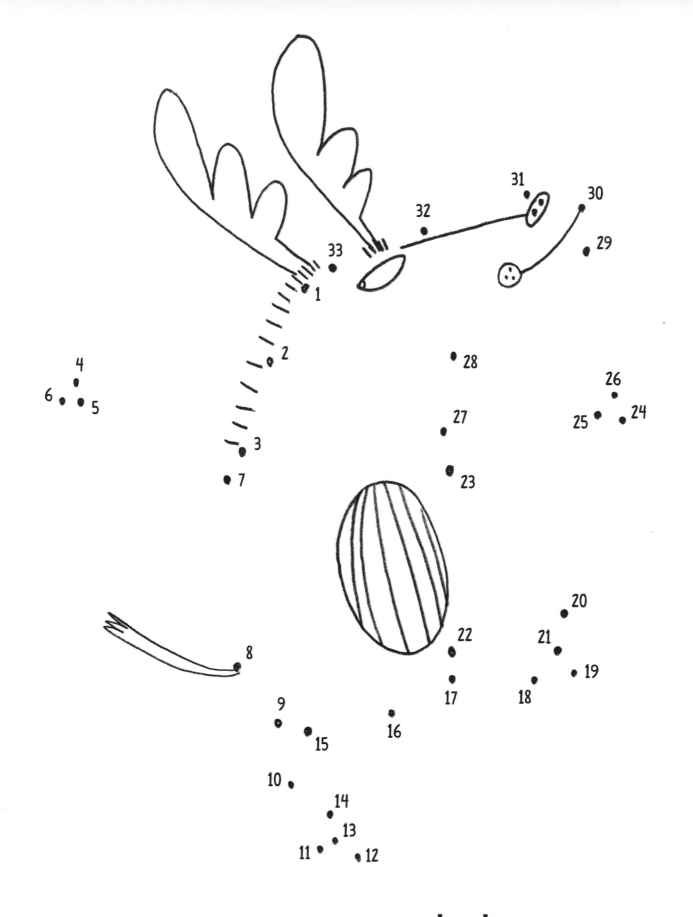

Ice-sculpture **contest**!
Connect the dots to see the winning sculpture.

This turkey is escaping! Give it **feathers** to help it fly away.

Color the **costume** of Super Santa Claus.

Draw the ugliest Christmas **sweater** you can imagine.

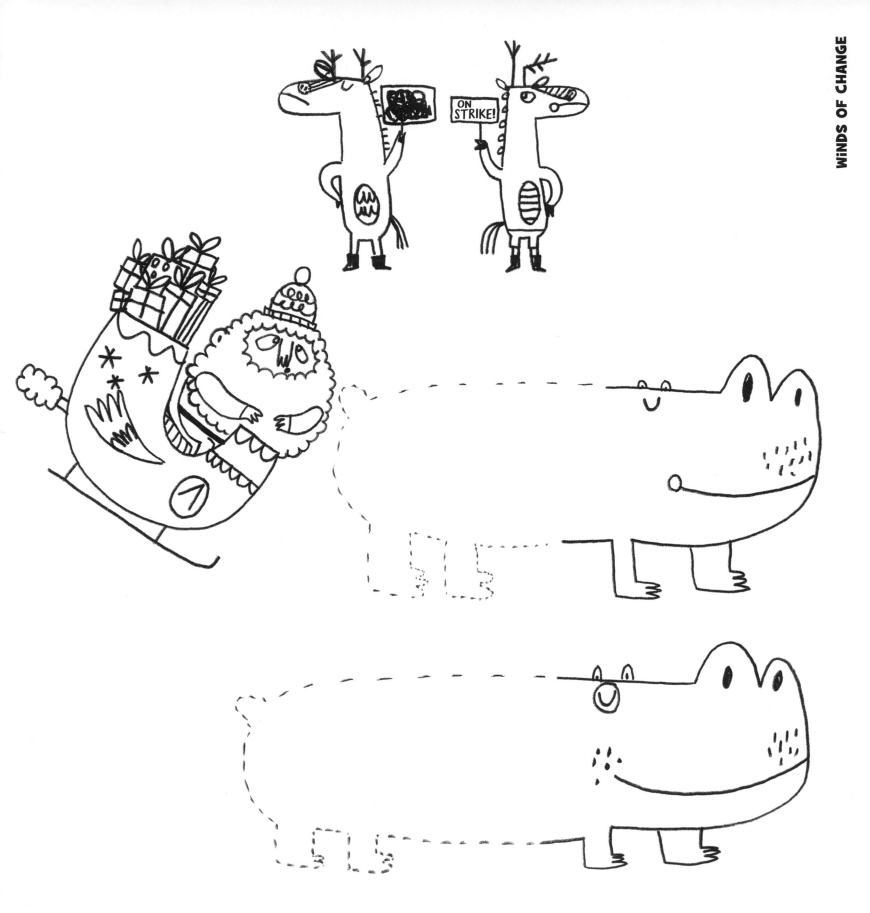

The reindeer don't want to work!
Finish the **hippos** so they can pull the sleigh.

The elves are lost in the forest.

Help them find their way home.

Draw a super-fast **motorbike** for Santa.

You forgot about the turkey!
Draw a big cloud of smoke coming from the **oven**.

The **fridge** was robbed!
Color the mess left behind.

Who do you think did it? Color him in red.

Someone threw **oysters** all over
the perfectly set table! Add some fish and snails.

Santa is out in the sun.
He might get too hot. Cut the page to give him **shorts**.

Draw something very **foolish**.
Don't worry, Santa will come by anyway.

Times are tough for turkeys!

Help them finish barricading their house
to protect them from being eaten.

Time passes. Add more spiderwebs taking over the tree.

Make the **snowman** melt!
Draw a big sun in the sky.

Decide which silly elves played a **joke** on Santa.

Draw the most delicious **gingerbread house** you can think of.

Snowball fight! Tear out this page,
then cut out the strips of paper and
scrunch them into balls to protect yourself.

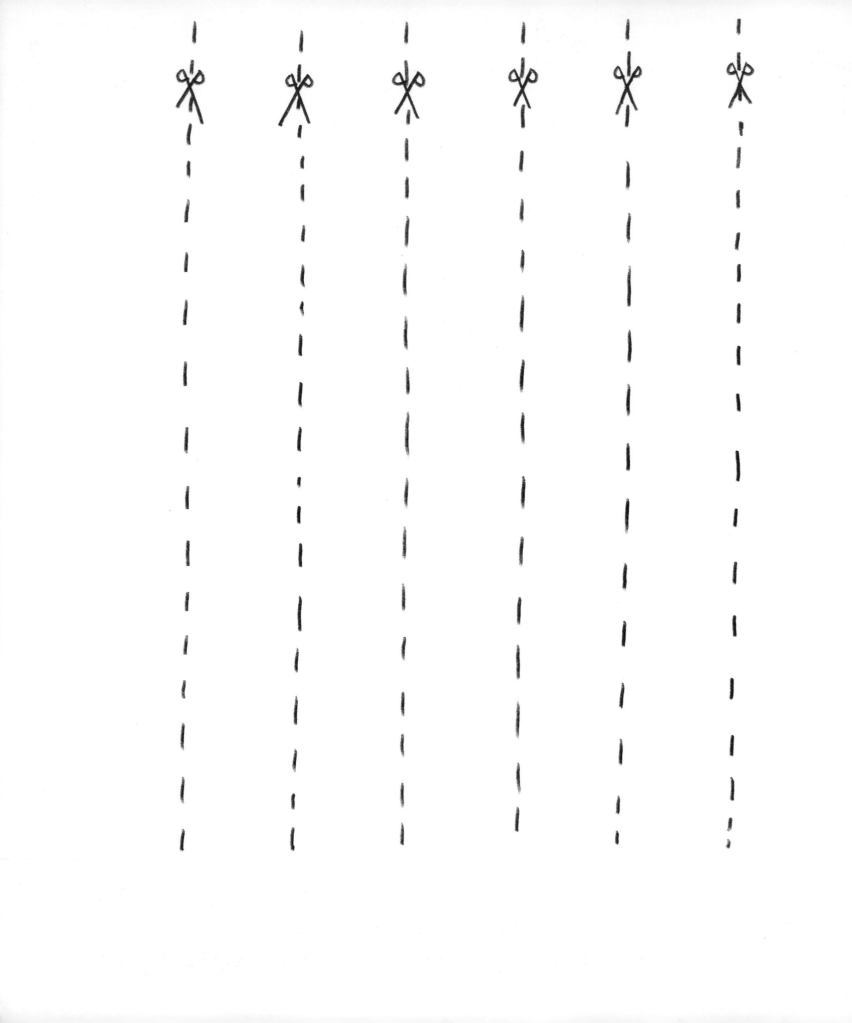

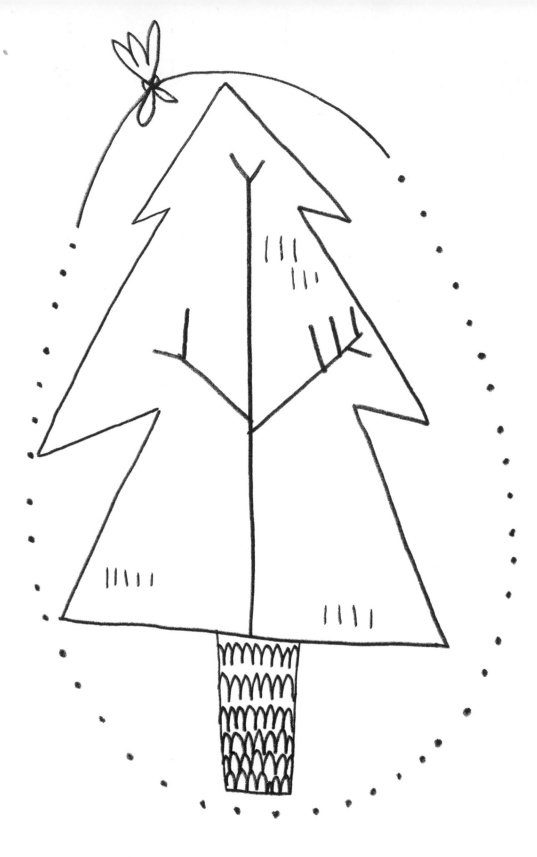

Christmas is far away! Finish bagging up the tree,
then cut out the page and scrunch it into
a nice ball before throwing it in the **recycling** bin.

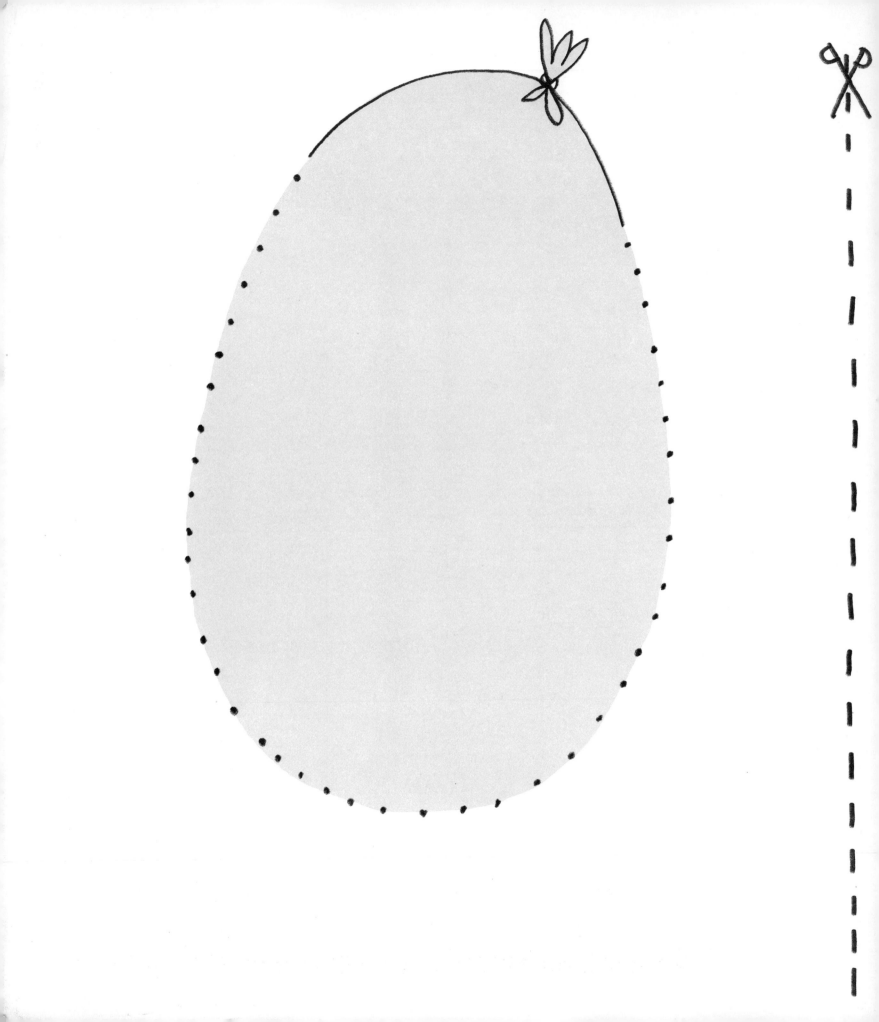